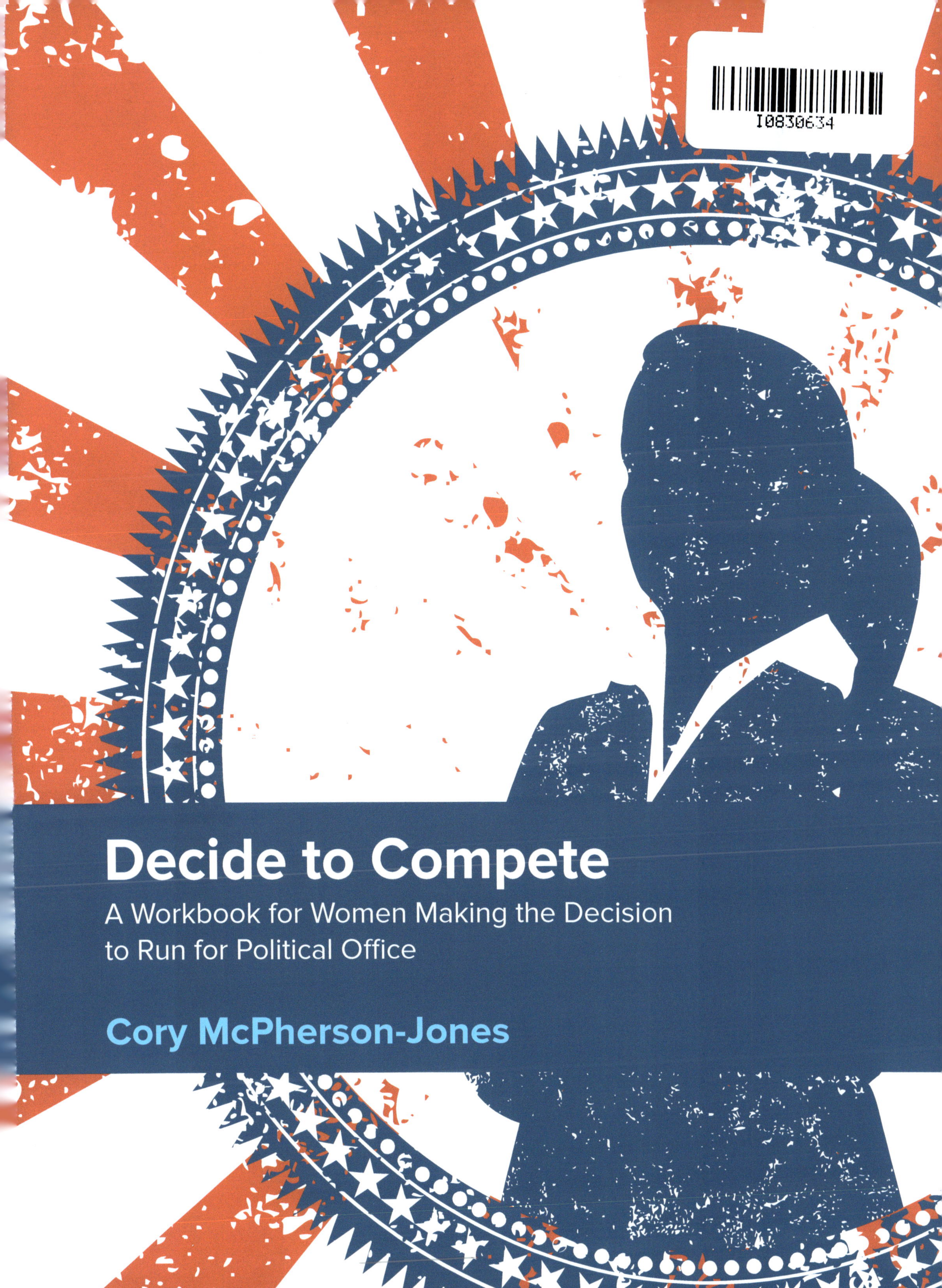

Decide to Compete

A Workbook for Women Making the Decision to Run for Political Office

Cory McPherson-Jones

Table of Contents

Introduction

I have two goals. The first is to increase the numbers of women in public office so that in the future, women will hold half of the political offices in the country. My second goal is to encourage you to run for public office, to provide you with questions that will lead you to your decision, and provide successful organizing and mentoring tools that will help you run a successful campaign.

A year after Hillary Rodham Clinton lost the presidential election on November 9, 2016, she and others are still evaluating the reasons that made this election so much different than others and whether having fewer women serving in public office, fewer women in the pipeline, and sexism played a role in her defeat. Recently, in the 2017 elections, more Democratic women ran and won against Republican candidates in local elections so her loss and President Trump's election triggered more women to run for office. It's called the "Hillary Effect." I hope you will consider running after completing the questions in this workbook.

Having more women in public office is meaningful to me because I believe in equal representation between men and women. It is important because women are not proportionately represented in political offices at the federal, state, and local level. Having more women in political office should bring women's experiences, interests, and problems more into focus and will hopefully include public policies and legislation related to women and children.

Hillary Clinton's candidacy gave me hope that women would be represented at the presidential level. Clinton faced many issues and you likely will too: media stereotypes, hostile language, communication styles, and criticism. In addition, she also faced Russian interference on behalf of Trump, release of the DNC and Podesta emails, the FBI Director James Comey announcements, the use of fake ads and articles on Facebook and Twitter, and the media's focus on her emails. Your campaign must be prepared for the unexpected issues that you will face. Hopefully, with time, awareness, and more women running for office, these obstacles and issues will be overcome. But even if they are not, women will be encouraged to disregard these obstacles, work around them, and run anyway.

Throughout the workbook, I have asked questions that have been identified as some of the barriers to women running for office and some of the most effective tools and successes that women who have been elected to public office have used that you will need to consider in your decision to run for office and be a successful political candidate. **Decide to compete!**

The State of Women In Politics

The numbers of women in elective office have increased over the years. But in 2018, women are still not equal to men. The Center for American Women and Politics show that:

In the U.S. Congress in 2018, "women hold 106, or 19.8%, of the 535 seats in the 114th U.S. Congress – 22, or 22.0%, of the 100 seats in the Senate, and 84, or 19.3%, of the 435 seats in the House of Representatives." Nancy Pelosi (D-CA) was the first woman in history to serve as Speaker of the House and now serves as minority leader. Women would need 28 more seats in the Senate and 134 in the House to achieve equal representation.

In Statewide Elective Executive Offices, which include Governors and Lt. Governors, in 2018, "71 women hold statewide elective offices across the country; women hold 22.8% of the 312 available positions." In state legislator positions in 2018, "1,871, or 25.3%, of the 7,383 state legislators in the United States are women. Women hold 446, or 22.6%, of the 1,972 state senate seats and 1,425, or 26.3%, of the 5,411 state house seats. Since 1971, the number of women serving in state legislatures has more than quintupled."

"As of February 2017, per the U.S. Conference of Mayors, of the 284 mayors of U.S. cities with populations 100,000 and over, 58, or 20.4%, were women. Of the 1,362 mayors with populations 30,000 and above, 286, or 21.0% were women."

– Statistics from CAWPI Center for American Women and Politics, "Women in Elective Office 2018." Rutgers Eagleton Institute of Politics, 9 Mar. 2018 www.cawprutgers.edu/.

To achieve equal representation

Women would need **28** **more seats in the Senate**

and **134** **in the House.**

Why am I interested in running for public office?

Why would I be a good candidate?

"If you don't have a seat at the table, you're probably on the menu. Washington works for those who have power. And no one gives up power easily, no one…Nobody's just going to say 'women have arrived and let's just move over'…We have a chance but we have to fight for it."

ELIZABETH WARREN

Identify my qualifications for public office.

Identify my personal characteristics that will support my candidacy and in political office.

What are the issues in my community that interest me the most?

Assessing Readiness

Do I have experience and knowledge about these issues that will contribute to their resolution? If so, what are they?

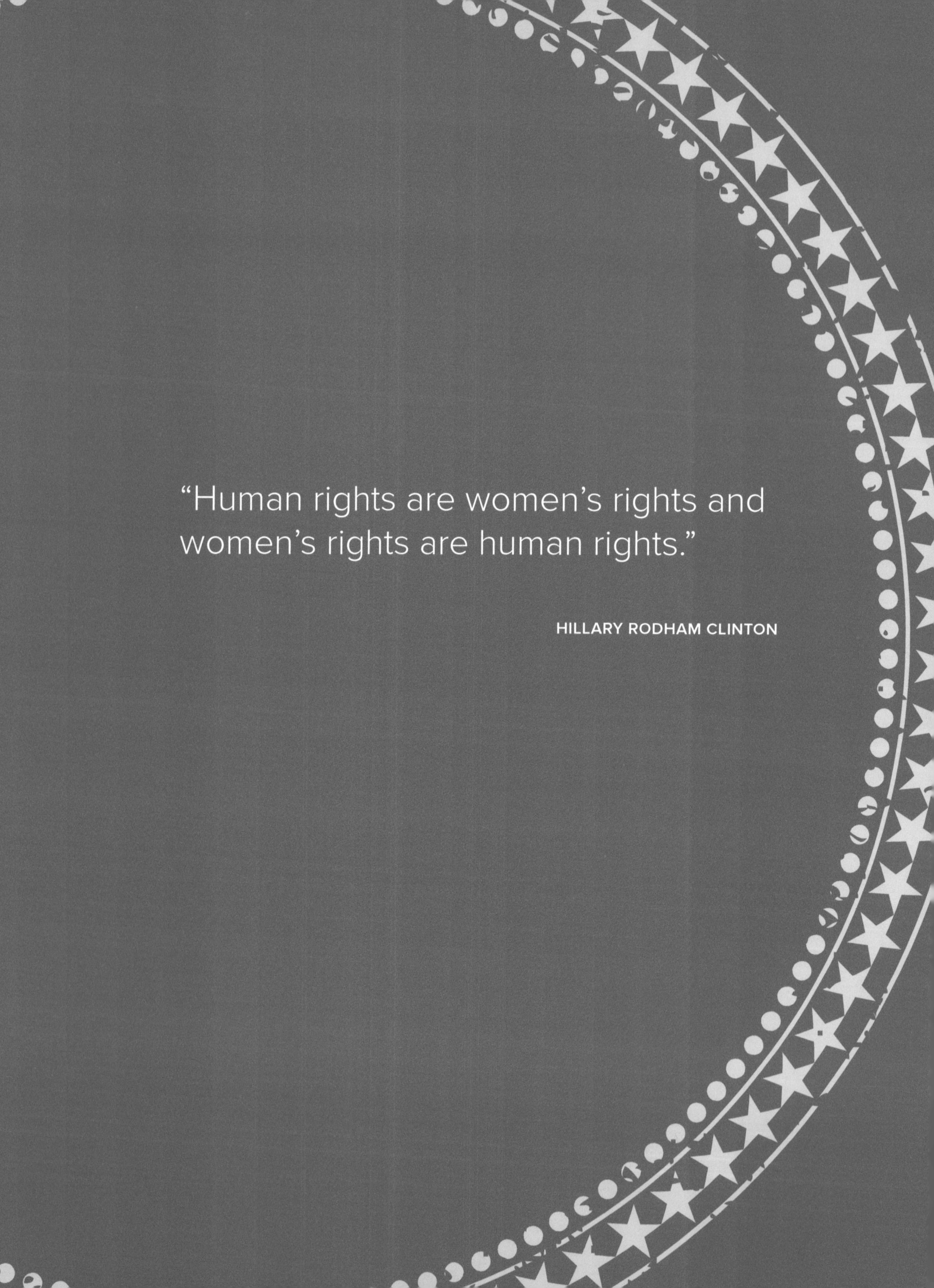
"Human rights are women's rights and women's rights are human rights."

HILLARY RODHAM CLINTON

Do I have contacts that have knowledge about these issues that I can learn from?

What are my values concerning politics and government?

Assessing Readiness

How capable do I feel that I can make a difference?

List any obstacles that would prevent me from my running for public office?

"For me, a better democracy is a democracy where women do not only have the right to vote and to elect but to be elected."

MICHELE BACHELET

How can I overcome these obstacles and get advice for how to deal with them?

Is there anything in my past that would prohibit me from running for office?

How can I overcome these obstacles and get advice as to how to deal with these issues?

How does being a woman help my potential candidacy?

Confronting Sexism, Gender Stereotyping, Racism, Anti-LGBTQ

What are some ways that sexism and gender stereotyping can impact my candidacy for office and if I win political office?

Clothes/Hair/Makeup, Voice/Pitch, Positions and Issues, Speeches/Communication, Intellect, Family, Unknown

Confronting Sexism, Gender Stereotyping, Racism, Anti-LGBTQ

How does being a minority and/or LGBTQ woman help my potential candidacy?

How does being a minority and/or LGBTQ woman possibly hurt my potential candidacy?

Discuss my ability to deal with criticism, misquotes, and unfair assessments of positions and campaign.

"I could not, at any age, be content to take my place by the fireside and simply look on. Life was meant to be lived. Curiosity must be kept alive. One must never, for whatever reason, turn his back on life."

ELEANOR ROOSEVELT

Can I be a woman who focuses on women's policy positions/issues in my campaign and in office?

★ Support, Mentors, Expertise

Who are my closest women and male friends who can support me and give me honest feedback on my possible candidacy for public office and the issues?

____

____

____

____

____

____

____

____

____

____

____

____

____

____

____

____

Support, Mentors, Expertise

Who are the people who can guide and mentor me throughout a candidacy for public office?

____

____

____

____

____

____

____

____

____

____

____

____

____

____

____

____

Who are the experts that I can call to learn the details of running for office, the law, policy positions, and government?

Support, Mentors, Expertise

Which of these classes can I take to help me learn about running for office?

- ◯ Run for Something: runforsomething.net
- ◯ Emily's List: emilyslist.org
- ◯ Democratic National Committee: traindemocrats.org
- ◯ She Should Run: sheshouldrun.org

Will my family be supportive of my work and travel schedule?

Who will provide full-time, part-time, or temporary child care assistance if and when needed?

Work/Life Balance

Who will help me with household responsibilities like cleaning, cooking, errands, driving children to activities and school, and helping them with homework?

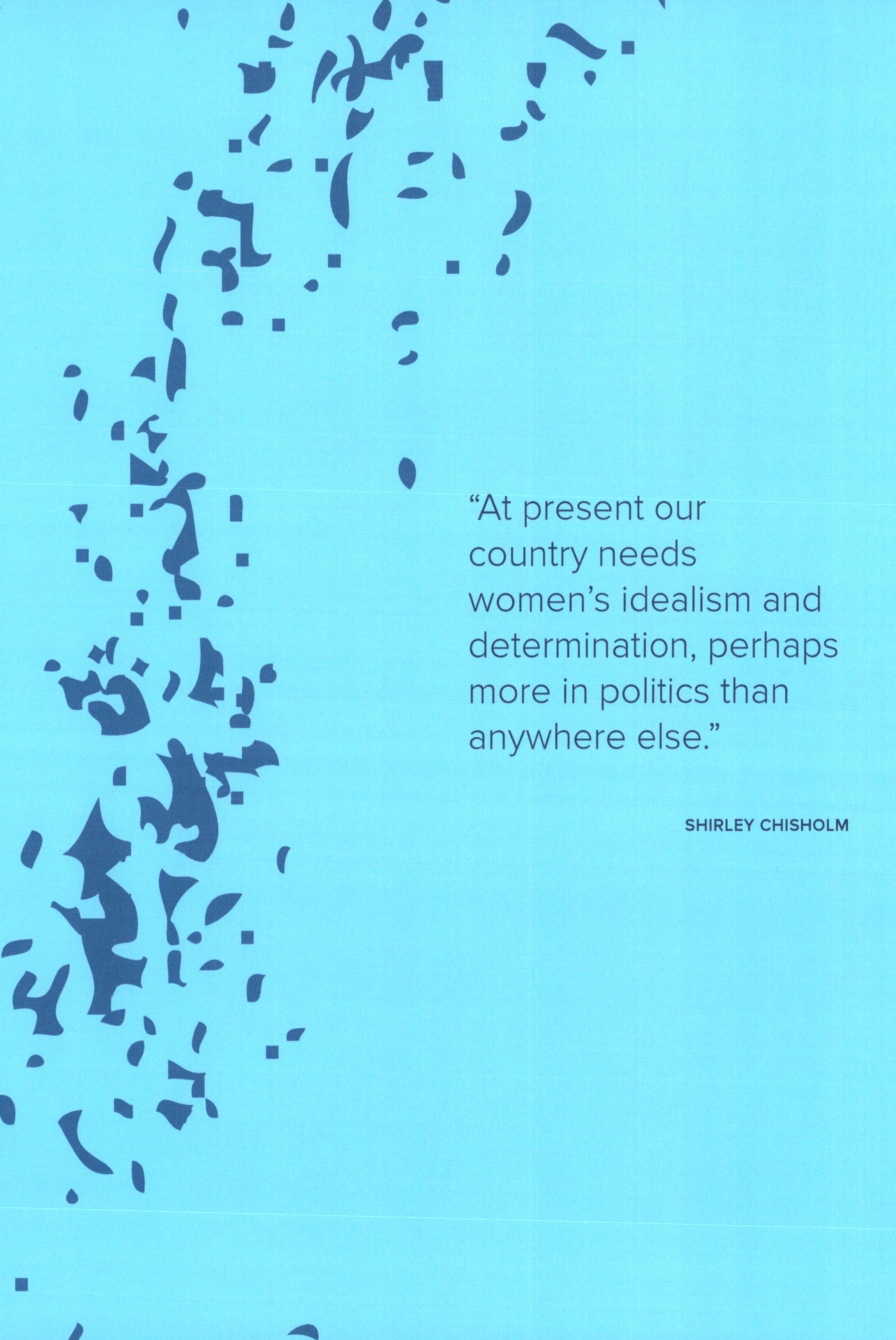

"At present our country needs women's idealism and determination, perhaps more in politics than anywhere else."

SHIRLEY CHISHOLM

Endorcement Possibilities

List the businesses in your community where you are considering running for office.

Unions, Politicians, Nonprofits.

Do I have any connections from these individuals or groups?

Endorcement Possibilities

Do I have any business relationships or friends who can connect me with these individuals or groups?

Endorcement Possibilities

What are the requirements for asking for endorsements?

What research do I need to do to find races open to me at the local, state, and federal level?

Evaluating Races

What race am I most qualified to run and is most likely to cover the issues that I am most interested and knowledgeable in?

What are the facts about my community, businesses, and constituents?

What are the main issues affecting the community that I am considering running in?

Campaign Team

Who are some possible candidates for the positions of:

Election lawyer

Communications

Social Media/Digital

Fundraising/Financial

Outreach/Organizing

Policy Positions/
Research

What is my message to potential voters:

How will I make sure the message is shared:

My campaign website ______________________________

Twitter

Facebook

Speeches

Headshots

Buttons, Flyers,
Posters, T-shirts

Fundraising Plan

Who will I go to for funding:

Myself

____

____

____

Friends

____

____

Family

____

____

Supporters

____

____

Facebook and
Twitter Campaign

____

____

Business Owners

____

____

____

Fundraising Plan

Who will I go to for funding:

Nonprofits

____

____

____

PAC

____

____

____

Political Party

____

____

____

Unions

____

____

____

____

____

____

____

____

____

Where will I recruit volunteers:

Friends

Family

Supporters

Facebook and
Twitter Campaign
Outreach

Nonprofits

Unions

PROS:

____

____

____

____

____

____

____

____

____

____

____

____

____

____

____

CONS:

____

____

____

____

____

____

____

____

____

____

____

____

____

____

____

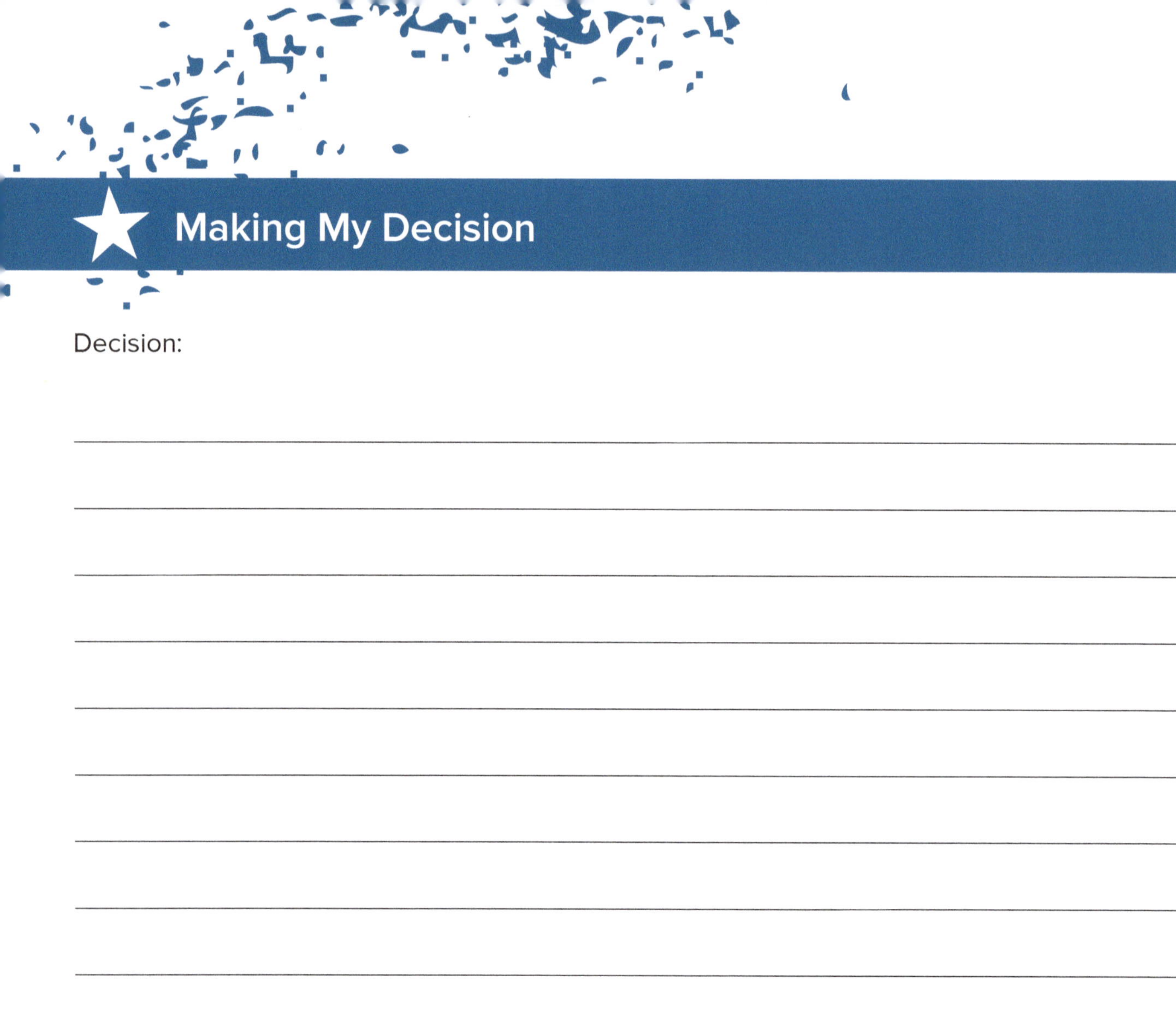

Making My Decision

Decision:

Resources

CAWP | Center for American Women and Politics. CAWP | Rutgers Eagleton Institute of Politics, 9 Mar. 2018, www.cawp.rutgers.edu/.

Clark, C., Clark J. (1984). The growth of women's candidacies for nontraditional political offices in New Mexico. *Studies in Soviet Thought*, 21(1), 57-65.

Crowder-Meyer, M.A. (2010). *Local parties, local candidates, and women's representation: How county parties affect who runs for and wins political office*. Princeton, NJ: Princeton University Press.

DesRoches, K. L., Clark, P. L., Hager, E., Larsen, S., Norelii, T., Pignatelli, D., & Shaheen, J. (2015). *Case studies of women in New Hampshire politics: an exploration of the barriers and supports for political candidates and incumbents*. Ann Arbor, MI: Proquest.

Doherty, L. (2011). Filling the female political pipeline: Assessing a mentor-based internship program. *Journal of Political Science Education*, 7(1), 34-47.

Dolan, K. (2008). Running against a woman: Do female opponents shape male candidate behaviors? *Social Science Quarterly*, 89(3), 765-779.

Fox, R.L. (2001). Gender and the decision to run for office. *Legislative Studies Quarterly*, 26(3), 411-435.

Fox, R. L., & Lawless, J. L. (2010). Gendered perceptions and political candidacies: A central barrier to women's equality in electoral politics. *American Journal of Political Science*, 55(1), 59-73.

Fox, R. L., & Lawless, J. L. (2014). Uncovering the origins of the gender gap in political ambition. *The American Political Science Review*, 108(3), 499-519.

Frederick, A. (2014). "Who better to do it than me!: Race, gender & the deciding to run accounts of political women in Texas. *Qualitative Sociology*, 37(3), 301-321.

Herrnson, P. S., Lay, J. C., & Stokes, A. K. (2003). Women running "as women": candidate gender, campaign issues, and voter-targeting strategies. *The Journal of Politics*, 65(1), 244-255.

Kaba, A. J. (2017). Educational attainment, citizenship, and black American women in elected and appointed national leadership positions. *The Review of Black Political Economy*, 44(1-2), 99-136.

Lawless, J., & Fox, R. (1999). Women candidates in Kenya. *Women & Politics*, 20(4), 49-76.

Litman, Amanda. *Run for Something: A Real-Talk Guide to Fixing the System Yourself.* Atria, 2017.

Meeks, L. (2012). Is she "man enough"? Women candidates, executive political offices, and news coverage. *Journal of Communication*, 62(1), 175-193.

Sanbonmatsu, K. (2006). Gender Pools and Puzzles: Charting a "Woman's Path" to the Legislature. *Politics & Gender*, 2(03).

Silbermann, R. (2015). Gender roles, work-life balance, and running for office. *Quarterly Journal of Political Science*, 10(2), 123.

Sottile, A. (2017). Meet the women inspired to run for office after the 2016 election. *Rolling Stone* Web. 22 Oct. 2017, www.rollingstone.com.

**Decide to Compete: A Workbook for Women
Making the Decision to Run for Political Office**

Acknowledgment
*Thank you to Nicole Pérez for her
design expertise and support.*

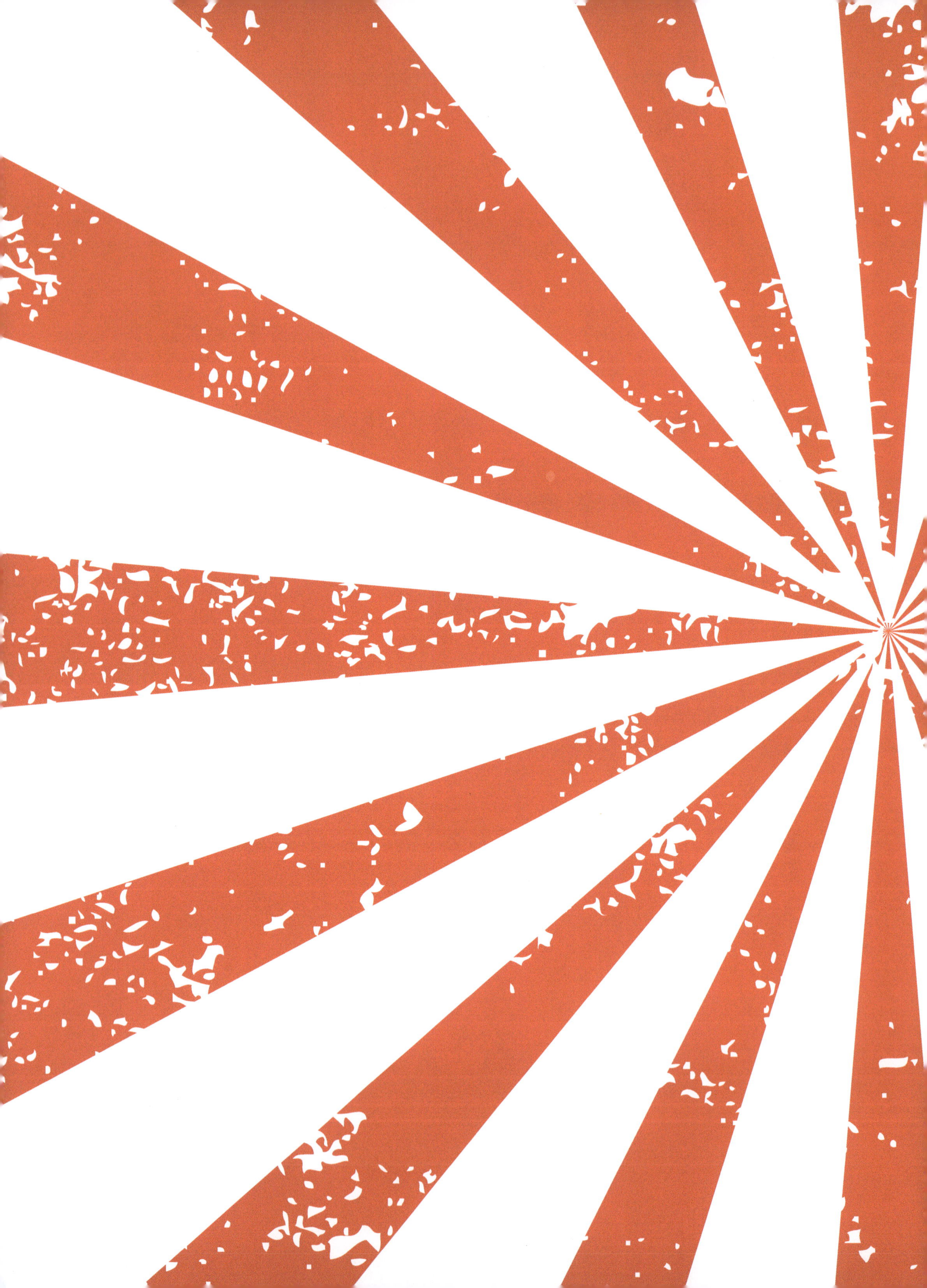